How to Analyze People

Analyze People Instantly Using Psychological Techniques, Social Skills, and Body Language Signals

By Simon King

"The human body is the best picture of the human soul. "

Ludwig Wittgenstein

Table of Contents

Introduction

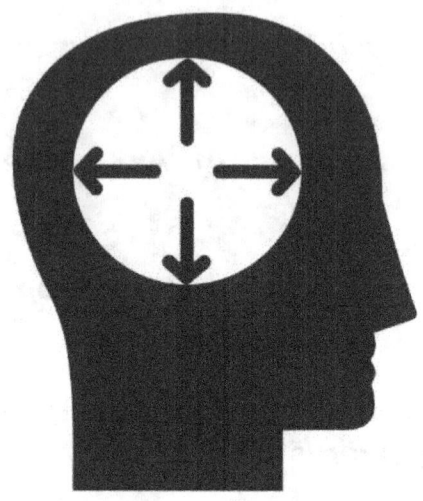

The gift to accurately read people is a gift that few people possess. Sure, some people think they have the gift, but there is no real basis for their belief. In all reality, in order to ready people accurately, you have to develop the skill.

It's true, the ability to read people certainly can be considered a gift, but it's not something that some people have and others do not. In fact, anyone can learn how to read people with the right training and practice.

Now, you may be wondering what the benefit is to reading people, and the answer is simple.

If you can read another person accurately, you can learn many things about them they may or may not share with you on their own. Not only can you accurately read things about their past and determine the kind of people they are, but you can also gauge how you should behave around them, and how you ought to react to the things they say and do.

Depending on the situation, this can give you great leverage in the relationship, and keep you one step ahead of the game.

Of course, this doesn't mean that you are always out to get something from the people you meet, but it does mean that you have the opportunity to always be that person who knows just what to do to say.

Effectively reading people can come in handy in many different parts of your life. From your job ambitions to your romantic aspects, being able to analyze the people around you is going to tell you exactly what you ought to do next.

This will not only give you a leg up on all your competition, it's going to set you apart as the number one choice in every realm.

So, how do you do it? How do you effectively learn how to analyze people?

The answer may surprise you, and in this book, I am going to show you how. Come with me and learn how to accurately analyze the people around you using scientific methods that have been proven to work.

By the time you reach the end of this book you will be a master of analytics, and know exactly what everyone around you is thinking, regardless of the situation you are in.

There is much to learn, so let's get started.

Chapter 1 – Analysis 101: An Overview

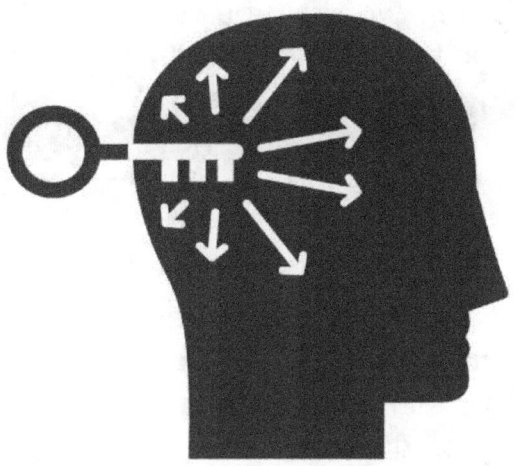

Before you can expect yourself to become an expert in the field of analysis, you first must understand what it is.

In this chapter, we are going to take an in-depth look at what analysis is, and how you can use it to benefit yourself in day to day life. Then, in the chapters to come, I am going to show you how to effectively practice analysis yourself, and develop the skill in your own life.

At its most basic definition, the analysis is the detailed study of an item or being with the intent of drawing a conclusion from that study.

In other words, you aren't just watching people for the sake of watching them, you are watching them with intent. There are things you wish to learn and have full intention of learning by watching the things they do.

Your motive behind this may be entirely unique and one that only you knows or understands, but the analysis process is going to be the same regardless of the motive you have behind doing it.

When it comes to people, you are going to use analysis to both understand why people behave the way they do and draw conclusions on how they are likely to behave in the future.

This will give you the upper hand in any and all interactions you have with this individual, and better prepare you to be the person you wish to be when you are around them.

It is important to note, however, that analysis isn't going to benefit you simply

because it shows you how other people operate.

A person who is good at analyzing others has multiple gifts. Gifts that you will learn to develop the more you learn how to analyze.

You might already possess some of these gifts, but even if you don't, you can rest assured that focusing on developing your analysis skills will sharpen these other traits as well.

But are you cut out to be an analyst? What are the skills or traits an analyst possesses?

Though some people are naturally better at analysis than others, anyone can learn how to do it. But before you dive into the exercises which will launch you into the field, let's take a second to study what skills an analyst often possesses.

You may have some of these skills, you may have all of these skills.

Or perhaps, you don't have any. Regardless, you need to work on developing each of them if you hope to master analysis.

What does an analyst look like?

The analyst is attentive, pays attention to detail, and knows how to handle the world around him. He isn't taken by surprise because he knows how the people around him behave, and how he expects them to behave in the future.

A person who excels at analysis isn't high strung, and he takes life as it comes, one step at a time.

Now, this is not to say that if you are an emotional person right now that you can't become good at analysis, but it is important to note that if you are an emotional person right now, you must get a grip on your emotions and learn how to control yourself before you can excel in this work.

Don't be swayed by your emotions. Don't be governed by the things that you see. If you are going to truly analyze those around you, you must do so objectively, without allowing yourself to get drawn into the moment.

Why would anyone want to analyze others?

If you spend much time in this hobby, or if you ever talk to anyone about what you do, you are certain to run into the question of "why?"

Some may look down on you as manipulative. Others may accuse you of using people or not being genuine.

Others may think you are always trying to analyze them and may make an effort to "throw you off", but regardless of what anyone else says, you may be wondering yourself why analysis is such a good thing to do.

First of all, many people are putting up a front. Most people in life want to project an image – a picture of themselves though it is far from the truth. If you are good at analysis, you will be able to see through this and understand what these people are really like.

This is going to make you a lot less gullible, and a lot harder to manipulate.

Secondly, you can learn a lot about a person through analysis, eliminating the need for pointless chatter or awkward situations. Of course, it can get just as awkward if you are always announcing that you already know things about them they haven't told you yet, but you get my point.

Finally, if you are good at analysis, you are better able to control yourself. You can accurately predict how a person is going to respond, and base your own response on this prediction. You can keep yourself one step ahead of the rest without much trouble at all, and you can always be prepared for what's next.

There are many reasons a person could want to engage in analysis, and really, your motives are your own.

Let's move on into the method behind the madness now, and break down the different components of human analysis. Take your time as you work through these, and practice each one separately.

We'll put them together in the end, and you will be able to analyze anyone you meet, whenever, wherever.

Chapter 2 – Analysis and Psychological Skills

By now, you know you want to analyze people, and you have your own reasons for wishing to do so. But, when it comes to analysis, you can't just simply go with what you think someone is doing, or base your deductions on why you would be behaving a certain way if it were you.

No, if you want to become a master of analysis, you must learn how to effectively analyze people using psychology. Though every person – and every mind – is unique, behavior is still behavior, and in general, people are going to behave the way they do for very specific reasons.

And this is where psychology comes in. The human mind is so vast and so incredible people have dedicated their lives to the study of it, and what they have found can be applied to a variety of other people and situations.

That's right. If you want to master analysis, you must first understand and sharpen your hand in psychology.

Psychology is the study of the human mind and general behavior – especially when that behavior is in a given context.

Now, if you were to simply try to break into the study of psychology, you would be almost instantly overwhelmed with all the options you have available. There are hundreds of sub-branches in the field and more things you could study than you could possibly have time for.

Since we are focusing on analysis, it is important to study the right field of psychology. As a general rule, studying how people behave in social situations is more than adequate for what you need.

You see, though many people strive to stand out from the crowd, and many people feel that they are entirely unique when it comes down to base human behavior, we are all more alike than many of us would like to admit. There are some things that are simply born into us that we can't help but do and that you can notice and analyze.

Some of these things include:

- **how we act when the opposite gender is present**

- **how we behave when we are with our peer group versus alone**

- **how we behave when we are trying to impress someone present**

- **how we behave when we are singled out of a crowd**

- **and more**

Learn which situations you are most interested in, and what you can gain from learning these things about a person. Apply them to the people you see, and effectively draw conclusions from a variety of situations.

Example number 1:

A person who is among a group of friends, or even a group of people they don't know is more likely to behave boldly than a person who is singled out from a crowd.

In one study, it was discovered that people who get a strike when bowling will only smile if they are with a group of people – and only after they turn to face the group.

In another study, children who were dressed for Halloween and together in a group all reportedly took more candy than if each individual child was called forward and asked to give his name before being allowed to take candy. In both situations, the children were told to take as much candy as they wanted.

Example number 2:

A person is more likely to do harmful or illogical things to conform to the people around them.

Studies prove that a person is more likely to engage in what appears to be a dangerous trick when more than one volunteer is chosen by the magician.

Studies also show that people are more likely to do things such as skydiving or base jumping when they are with a group rather than when they go solo.

On the other hand, you can use psychology to guard your own mind when you are analyzing people.

After all, studies show that when you are attracted to a person for any reason, you are bound to put positive connotations on everything they do, regardless of what that action is.

This is why many people find themselves stuck in toxic relationships or doing things for people that others consider irrational or downright crazy.

But how do I tie psychology to analysis.

There are times when it can be difficult to decide what to study, but at the end of the day, you need to choose what you want to know about a person. If you are hoping to analyze the recruiter in a job interview, you need to study the field of body language.

If you are hoping to analyze how your date feels, you need to study body language as well as how the opposite gender behaves in situations they don't feel comfortable.

As an analyst, you have to be smart. This means you need to do your own homework on the field of interest, then study what you need to get the information you need. A large part of being an effective analyst is staying one step ahead of the rest of the crowd.

When you understand how the crowd works, you are in an even better position to analyze.

Now, you may be wondering how this is going to help you with analysis.

The answer is simple. When you understand how people behave in certain situations (based on your study of psychology) you will be able to deduce specific things about them.

For example:

If you know that a person is outgoing in certain social situations and timid in others, you can accurately predict how they are going to react based on the situation they are placed in.

You can use this to your advantage in various realms:

If you are trying to land a promotion in your company, invite the hiring manager out to a social situation you know he will be more open in. This will place you in a positive situation in his mind and put you in a better position for the job.

Or,

If you are trying to make a good impression on a date, and you want to get to know your partner in a more outgoing way, take them somewhere casual where there are a lot of people present, rather than a place where they will be in the spotlight.

Observe how they react, and get a glimpse into how they genuinely are on the inside. Use psychology to analyze their reactions.

Chapter 3 – The Body Language Secret Revealed: Signals Vs. Words

People can say what they want, but the true measure of what a person is feeling can be found in their body language. Body language is how a person presents themselves while they are doing something. This can be something as simple as having a conversation, or what they do when they are performing or giving a speech.

When it comes to proper analysis, you must learn how to read body language properly. The micro and macro expressions people make can be so subtle it's nearly impossible for you to pick them up unless you are well versed in the study.

However, learning how to read body language requires time and dedication, as well as the practice of your skills.

Too many times, the assumption that "when a person does this it automatically means this" reigns supreme in the study of body language, but this rule of thumb can be very misleading.

For example, a smile is not a smile.

What I mean is that just because a person may be smiling, it doesn't mean that they are happy with the situation. Many people – especially women – will smile for a variety of reason, even when they aren't comfortable with the situation.

When you analyze, don't fall take your subject at face value. Study them.

When someone smiles, don't look at their lips, look at their eyes. A genuine smile uses different muscles than a fake smile and will cause the skin to the eyes to wrinkle. If a person is smiling and there are no wrinkles (or rather, crow's feet), then the smile isn't genuine.

Don't misinterpret physical contact, either.

Many people associate a physical contact with affection. A light brush on the arm is flirty, putting your hand on someone in public shows that you care for them.

But, this may not be the case, and affection is not something you want to automatically deduce from physical contact. Studies have proven that men will often touch women – even a light touch on the arm or pat on the back – to show dominance, and waitresses – both genders – who touch lightly when they place the bill on the table are far more likely to get a higher tip.

Now, let's turn out attention to words.

Though you are able to read people – and often more accurately – through body language, we must not forget verbal communication when it comes to analysis.

We as people are constantly communicating with our words. From the people we run into at the grocery store to the close friends we chat with for hours on end, words flood our lives.

But, it's time to let go of the stereotypes we associate with verbal communication – the biggest of which being whether it's possible to detect lying.

There are tons of stereotypes and alleged tricks associated with lying, each one promising that you will be able to detect deceit over the truth with "foolproof" steps.

However, studies have effectively shown that being able to detect a lie watching body language or listening to verbal tone is nearly impossible. Even lie detectors have been known to miss-detect frequently.

Another stereotype we must cease to follow is the thought that "uhs" automatically point to nervousness.

That's right. Though we were all taught in grade school to never fill empty speech with filler words, it's time to let go of that stereotype, and stop reducing nervousness from those we speak to.

Studies have shown that speakers who use filler words in their speeches often receive higher ratings because their speeches tend to sound more fluid than those with empty space between words.

If you want to effectively analyze people, stop trying to pick the lies from the truths and spend your energy in other realms that are far more productive.

One of the biggest mistakes analytics make is to associate negativity with their analysis.

For example:

If a person is quiet they must be hiding something.

Or,

If a person avoids eye contact they must be lying.

Or,

If a person uses a lot of filler words they must be nervous.

Instead, use your analysis to accurately deduce conclusions from the people you are studying.

When using body language to analyze, choose to look at the person as a whole. Analyze how genuine their smile is. Analyze how fluid they move. If they are stiff, jumpy, or using fake smiles – then you can deduce they are nervous or under stress.

So what can we take away from our study of body language?

To put it in a nutshell, consider these things:

- Look at the eyes when you analyze a smile.

- Don't assume affection when you analyze physical contact between two people.

- Stop wasting your time and efforts trying to detect lies, put the energy into more productive matters.

- Stop assuming that a person who uses filler words is nervous or forgetful

- It's much more accurate to analyze a person's entirety than it is to try to pick out the subtle cues – everyone is different, and at a first meeting, it is nearly impossible to distinguish someone who is being flirty versus someone who is mere 'a toucher'.

Chapter 4 – Science Vs. Fiction: Five Real Life Personalities You Can Effectively Analyze Today

In the last chapter, I warned you not to jump to conclusions about body language, and I reminded you to let go of the negative connotations we tend to place on the world around us.

Stop assuming the worst in people, and never assume that a person is doing something maliciously without any true foundation for your assumption. You will find letting go of these things will alone help your analysis out immensely.

But, this is only part of the step. The analysis is a two-way street in which you must seamlessly blend not doing some things and actively doing others. In this chapter, I am going to show you the 5 most common personality traits you will run into as you analyze people, and give you deductions you can effectively gather from these people.

Experience Seekers

You can spot these people by their openness to new situations. They aren't afraid to try things that are new, and they aren't afraid to be the first people to do things. These people tend to have an appreciation of art and are very much in touch with their emotions.

You will hear these people speak of how they feel, express interest and an appreciation for creativity, and often comment on the beauty of the world or people around them.

What can you deduce from this?

An experience seeker is someone who holds unconventional beliefs. They enjoy going against the crowd, and this may be for the sheer sake of going against the crowd.

You can expect this person to find ways to be controversial, though they may not believe in what they are doing themselves.

Conscientious People

Conscientious people tend to be well organized. They see their daily tasks as their duties, and they stick with these duties until they have seen them through. You will notice these people become irritated when something happens that disrupts their days, making it more difficult for them to get things done.

You can spot these people easily, though they may not always be busy when you see them. There is a sense of organization about them, and they almost always seem to have somewhere to be.

What can you deduce from this?

A conscientious person is a person who gets things done. You can effectively deduce that this person is dependable, punctual, and only agrees to the plans they know they can keep.

You can also trust this person to mean what they say, no matter how brutally honest they are being.

Extroverts

Extraverts tend to fill their lives with a variety of hobbies, but not necessarily a depth of hobbies. You can consider these people to be the Jacks-of-all-Trades in society, but not a master of any.

They are seeking social thrills, and feed off the energy that is produced from a group of people. These people tend to be outgoing but not gregarious, though some may be. They look for social situations, even if they aren't going to be a part of them, simply because they feed off the energy.

Extraverts like to try new things, much like the Experience Seekers, but the things the extroverts are trying they aren't likely to stick with. It's the constant motion they are seeking, never sitting still.

What can you deduce from this?

Extraverts tend to be in the know. They know what the current trends are, they know what's popular, and they know the latest gossip. You can rest assured if there is anything you wish to know, these people will have the answers for you.

Be careful, however, as anyone who will do something with you is bound to do it to you, and you could find yourself the topic of his next gossip session.

The Agreeables

The agreeable person tends to get along with everyone. They try to make everyone happy, seeking to promote unity in a crowd. These people tend to say yes more often than no, and more willing to do a lot more to make people happy than others.

These people put other's needs above their own and are the kind of people who would give you the shirt off their backs. However, an agreeable person isn't always honest, as in their quest to promote harmony they may agree with things they don't believe.

What can you deduce from this?

You can trust an agreeable person to do their best to meet your needs, though you may find that they tend to be more of a doormat in their personalities. Though agreeable people tend to be the people who show up and get things done, they also tend to agree with more than they can keep up with.

Also keep in mind an agreeable person may not support what you are saying, though they say that they do.

Neurotics

Neurotic people are people who tend to experience and focus on negative emotions more than positive. These are the people who gravitate toward depression, anger, sorrow, and pointing out the bad in situations.

These people are extremely sensitive to what is going on around them and don't respond well to stress. They tend to take things personally and place a negative spin on any situation. These people also tend to overreact and find that even a mild rocking of their emotions is enough to make them feel like all is lost.

What can you deduce from this?

Neurotic people are easy to spot, but they aren't as easy to get to know. They tend to be closed off and focus on the bad that happens both in society and in their lives.

Everything is a really big deal to a person who is neurotic. A comment that is made, a bad experience they have, or even just reading a bad headline can send them into depression or anger with little or no warning.

So what does this all mean for an analyst?

You may wonder why these personality types matter, or why you would want to deduce such things about people. This is when you must remember that why a person is analyzing another is personal, and two people analyzing the same person could be doing so for entirely different reasons.

Though you are the only person who can answer why you are analyzing, these are the key things you can learn from these major personality traits. You may be able to shape your social circle built on these things, or you may be trying to find the right person to fill that position in your company.

Regardless, memorize these traits and put your analysis into practice. The more you practice, the easier it's going to be for you to pick up on these traits instantly, speeding your analysis to under a minute.

Chapter 5 – Life Application: Read People Instantly

Now, with all this information under our belts, it's time to put it into practice. In this final chapter, I want to teach you how to read people instantly, no matter what situation you find yourself in, how many people are there, or how well you know this person.

Remember that the act of reading people is a skill that needs to be developed, not one that you automatically have. This means you will need to put this final chapter into practice, and you will have to work at it before you can effectively trust your gut feeling on your reading.

Plan to spend a couple months on practice before you can be accurate in your readings.

It's also important to realize this is with daily practice, not half-hearted practice every few days. If you want to be good at reading people, you must put in the effort, or it simply isn't going to happen.

Okay, it's time we get into the step by step process you will use to analyze, then it will be up to you to make it happen.

Let's begin.

Start by taking in the entire situation.

You are often told that a person who has their arms crossed is closed off and doesn't want to be approached. But if the room is cold, or if they are sitting in a chair without armrests, this so-called "cue" doesn't really make sense.

Or, as we saw in the last chapter, personality must be taken into consideration. A person who is always jumpy will be jumpy in any situation. It's who they are. But, if that same person suddenly changes their behavior, then you need to figure out why.

After considering entire context, look for cues and clues that go together.

A person who is avoiding eye contact may lack self-esteem, but a person who isn't making eye contact, is constantly touching his face, who has sweaty palms of the forehead and also appears jittery – that person could well be lying or hiding something.

Also, consider your own personal feelings toward this person.

We all tend to form opinions about people within seconds of meeting them, and those opinions can taint how you analyze. If you decide you like someone (or if you are attracted to them in any way) a positive light will be shed on everything they do, even if it would otherwise seem questionable.

At the same time, if you decide you don't like someone for any reason, your opinion about them will be tainted.

41

You can try to be unbiased in your analysis, but you can't argue with your brain's predispositions. This isn't to say that you can't still read them accurately, but it does mean that you must be careful and take an honest analysis of what you see.

After all, there are social cues that all people give which can be read.

Before we get into the physical cues people give, here's a clue on how to study the appearance of someone.

When you choose a target to analyze, look at the person's appearance. Look for things such as tattoos, piercings, class rings, flashy clothing, and anything else considered "edgy".

Though in this modern world many people like to push off these methods of self-expression as completely irrelevant to the person doing it, science says otherwise. People who make permanent changes to themselves, or go out of their way to be flashy or showy are doing it for a reason.

They want to be perceived as something – and if you want to know what they wish to be perceived as simply look at what they are projecting. This isn't to say that they aren't genuine, or that you can't trust someone with an edgy or showy appearance, but it is a good clue that they like to put on a show.

It's then up to you to learn what that show is, and how they want to be perceived.

For example:

You're out to dinner in a nice, but not too nice, restaurant. Everyone is dressed casually until you see a group of friends come in. They all look roughly the same, except for the one that has the nicest clothes, the most defined hairstyle, and wears the nicest shoes.

Your initial thought may be that he has money – which is exactly what he wants you to think. And this is where your analysis begins.

Whether this man has money or not is irrelevant. What matters is the fact he wants you to assume that he does. This shows that money is important to him. This shows that appearances are important to him.

To feel important, he feels he must look like he has money, and odds are, to treat others with importance, he's likely to judge whether they have money first.

Do your homework on how people who focus on money feel and operate, and you have a fantastic baseline.

Of course, situations such as this are external. You sit back from afar and watch it take place, then make your analysis happen. But how do you analyze when a person is talking to you, or when you are in the middle of meeting someone?

How do you answer that age-old question of whether a person is manipulating you, or merely nervous?

If you are wondering whether a person is being genuine, consider this:

Consider how this person is speaking with you. Ask yourself if they are mimicking you, even subtly – are they speaking in the same way you are (tone, speed, phrases)? Are they using the same mannerisms?

People subconsciously mimic others when they feel in sync with them. It can be faked, of course, but it would be incredibly hard for someone to fake this for an entire situation.

Another cue to watch for is who wraps up the conversation, and how.

Busy schedules are constantly demanding we go one way or another, but you can still analyze how a person wraps up a conversation. Yes, they have to go and pick up the kids, but do they seem reluctant to leave? Do they proclaim how you need to stay (or get) in touch?

If so, the interaction was likely genuine. However, if they are clearly focused on what time it is, if they seem antsy or like they have their mind on other things, or if they appear relieved when they are leaving, it's likely the interaction wasn't as genuine as it may have appeared – and this includes situations in which they were laughing and talking, too.

It is also interesting to note that this same behavior will be seen even if you are the one who puts an end to the conversation. Even if you are the person who has to be elsewhere, study the other person when you close the conversation. The look of relief will still be present, the need for them to "get away".

Though subtle, you will begin to see just how many of these kinds of cues are given each and every time you are having an interaction with someone. These are the cues that you can rely on and analyze – and these are the cues which are hard to fake.

Understanding how the human mind works is a complex study, and it's going to take you months of practice before you are able to crack the case without much trouble, but trust me, with dedicated time and practice, you're going to get the hang of it, then any and all analysis will come as second nature.

To put it in a nutshell, what does this all mean?

When you are met with any real life situation and you wish to analyze those present, do these things:

- **Take a step back and look at the entire situation before you draw conclusions**

- **Analyze body language in its entirety before you decide what the person is feeling**

- **Try to remain as unbiased as possible when you are analyzing, however, keep in mind that you will still be biased to an extent**

- **Study how people present themselves – clues lie in tattoos, unnecessarily fancy clothing, flashiness, and edginess**

- **Analyze a person's actions as they are speaking with you – look for clues they like you**

- **Pay attention to how a conversation is wrapped up – who wraps it up first, and how.**

Conclusion

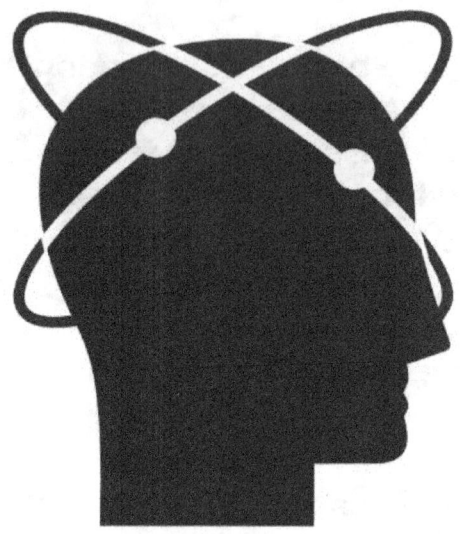

There you have it, everything you need to know about body language, analysis, and how to read people accurately and effectively. I hope this book was able to give you a thorough understanding of analysis, and show you what you have been doing wrong up to this point.

People make many mistakes when they try to analyze because they aren't basing any of their methods on facts. They see something that looks cool on some television series, and they try it out for themselves, only to discover that they are wrong time and time again.

But what Hollywood uses as analysis is far from fact, and unless you practice how to do it effectively, you are going to end with the same results as everyone else.

I hope this book was able to show you why those methods don't work, and why you need to change your approach to analysis if you want to do it accurately.

The next step is to put what you have learned into practice. I hope I emphasized enough how important the practice part of this skill is. You must practice daily, and you must be dedicated to getting results.

No one masters any skill by only trying it halfway, and the same goes for analysis. Take the methods you have read in this book, and start putting them into action today. Don't be afraid to make mistakes, don't be afraid to slip up, and don't be afraid to start again.

The only way you will get better is to put yourself into real life situations that allow you to practice, and when it comes to analysis, nothing can beat the hands-on experience.

So approach this skill with an open mind, a lot of patience, and dedicate yourself. You must be willing to put in the time and effort, and once you do, you will see the payoff. No one will be able to hide their thoughts from you, and you'll be able to choose your next move wisely.

Now get out there and read the world. There is so much to discover, and when you put yourself in the driver's seat, you will get the results you are hoping for.

P.S. Thank you for reading this book. If you've enjoyed this book, please don't shy, drop me a line, leave a review or both on Amazon. I love reading reviews and your opinion is extremely important for me.

My Amazon page:
www.amazon.com/author/kingsimon

Simon King has been a psychologist and mental health analyst for nearly two decades. His passion for the subject stems back to his childhood, and he has pursued both an educational and professional career in the field ever since.

Simon King has had the opportunity to take his studies overseas, where he spent several years in Switzerland, Germany, and England sharpening and adding to his knowledge before he eventually married and settled down with his wife, Melanie.

Melanie also studies psychology, and her added knowledge has helped Simon King in his line of work for many years. They moved back to the United States in 2005 and have both enjoyed successful careers and a happy marriage and family life with three children.

Writing a book has been on Simon King's mind for the past few years, and he is thrilled to finally have the opportunity to share some of his exquisite knowledge with the world. His greatest wish is that you will take this knowledge and enrich your own life, finding the same happiness and fulfillment he has.